Little Creek Press
A Division of Kristin Mitchell Design, LLC
5341 Sunny Ridge Road
Mineral Point, Wisconsin 53565

Limited First Edition
September 2011

For information or to order books:
Foundry Books
105 Commerce Street
Mineral Point, Wisconsin 53565
608.987.4363 • info@foundrybooks.com
or www.littlecreekpress.com

Library of Congress: 2011915846

ISBN-10: 0-9828023-6-6
ISBN-13: 978-0-9828023-6-6

Colleen Moore's
DOLL CASTLE

MADE BY RICH TOYS
with Related Toys and Books

CAROL STEVENSON

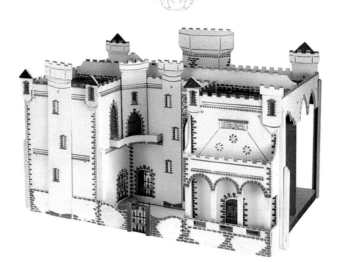

Photography by Chris Elinchev, Small Pond Productions

LITTLE CREEK PRESS
A DIVISION OF KRISTIN MITCHELL DESIGN, LLC
Mineral Point, Wisconsin

In memory of

Colleen Moore

1902 - 1988

the "Silent Star" still shines brightly…

A special thank you to...

JoAnn Belanger

Jean Gallin

Ann Mesnard

Sally and Tom McEnteer

Patricia Wehmeier

And to

Kristin Mitchell and Dana Gevelinger

of Little Creek Press who with the help of the Fairies

waved their technical wand and turned a simple

booklet into a magical book.

And

Chris Elinchev of Small Pond Productions

for his dazzling photography.

Colleen Moore's Fairy Castle. Photograph courtesy of JB Spector/Museum of Science and Industry, Chicago.

Once upon a time,

there was a little girl who had one blue eye and one brown eye. Her name was Kathleen Morrison, and like most little girls of the early 1900s she wanted to grow up to be a movie star. And she did! Her theatrical name became Colleen Moore.

Her film career lasted from 1917 to the mid-1930s, and she appeared or starred in over 60 films like *Sally*, *Flaming Youth*, *Ella Cinders*, and *Lilac Time*. During the 1920s she became one of First National Pictures most popular and extremely well-paid stars.

But there is another famous legacy associated with Colleen Moore. It is her fabulous Fairy Castle, which has enchanted millions of visitors to Chicago's Museum of Science and Industry where it has been on permanent display since 1949.

In 1925, while filming *The Desert Flower*, Miss Moore broke her neck. During the six weeks she was hospitalized, she became interested in crippled children and promised herself that someday she would do something to benefit them.

While on a cruise to Hawaii with her parents in 1928, Miss Moore's father, Charles Morrison, sensing her unhappiness over her failing first marriage, suggested building a fairy castle. It would actually be her seventh doll house and include her growing miniature collection. "This time, [her father said] let's get an architect and artists and build a work of art." *

When the Fairy Castle was completed in 1935, she called the Children's Hospital in Los Angeles and asked the volunteer association if they would like to have a "castle viewing" tea at her home in Bel Air to benefit the hospital. Jerry Fitzgerald, of the May Company's public relations department in Los Angeles, heard of the proposed tea and came up with the idea of a nationwide tour of department stores.

The tour initially included Macy's in New York, The Fair in Chicago and The May Company in Los Angeles. A private car on the Santa Fe Chief and the services of Railway Express successfully transported the Fairy Castle from city to city from 1935 to 1940, raising more than $650,000 for children's hospitals and charities.

This nationwide tour also became a merchandising tie-in opportunity for toy companies to sell related items. Effanbee's "Wee Patsy" became the Fairy Princess. Rich Toys provided a representational dollhouse version of the castle in three different sizes. Tootsietoy's dollhouse furnishings, although not very royal, were the right scale.

Silent Star, Colleen Moore, Doubleday & Co., 1968

The Toy Promotion

Copy of the ad in the *Chicago Tribune* on November 24, 1935, showing toys and books available when you visited The Fair to view the Colleen Moore Doll House.

The total cost for all five items illustrated was $3.75. In 1935, with the United States still in the midst of a severe financial depression, $3.75 was a substantial sum.

Over the years, I have been able to collect all five items, with some minor exceptions: my "Doll Castle" is the large eight room version, not the three room version shown in the ad at right, and my "Wee Patsy" came in a different box, not the one shown with extra outfits.

A postcard of The Fair. The eighth floor was devoted to toys and referred to as "Toyland."

This brochure was distributed by The Fair in 1935 to promote visiting the Doll House to raise money for crippled children. Admission to view the Doll House (which was later renamed the Fairy Castle) was 20 cents for adults, 10 cents for children. The brochure contains pictures and information and lists the 17 beneficiaries who were there to receive financial aid from the exhibition, e.g., Children's Memorial Hospital, Infant Welfare Society, etc. There is also a lengthy list of the members of the Women's Advisory Committee in Chicago. The brochure was given to me by Ann Mesnard of Chicago, a longtime friend and fellow collector.

A Collector's Quest

I imagine many children stand in front of Colleen Moore's Fairy Castle in the Museum of Science and Industry in Chicago and secretly wish they could take it home with them. It was not until 1974 that I discovered for a brief time in the 1930s there was a way to do that.

When Flora Gill Jacobs' book *Dolls' Houses in America* was published in 1974, I eagerly leafed through the pages. Lo and behold, there were pictures and a brief write-up titled *"A Commercially Made Colleen Moore Castle."* The one pictured was the large eight-room version that, along with Tootsietoy furnishings, had been purchased in 1934 at Marshall Field's in Chicago. The reference noted it was made by Rich Toys of Clinton, Iowa.

Needless to say, my reaction was "I've got to have one!" Being an inveterate flea market, garage sale, toy and doll show attendee, I felt confident I would soon run across this Doll Castle to take home for my very own. Wrong. It took almost twelve years to find one after finally advertising for it in *Collectors United*. There was only *one* response to my ad.

A dealer in Pittsburgh wrote that she had one for sale. A quick trip was put together in June 1986. As it turned out, her Doll Castle was in very good condition, with a few exceptions: an upstairs wall was missing, the courtyard fencing had been broken off, but miraculously saved, and the courtyard walkway was missing. The large window in the living room, the counterpart of the Great Hall in the Fairy Castle, was also missing.

However, still affixed was the all-important label, which reads "The Approved Colleen Moore Doll Castle a Rich Toy – Clinton, Iowa." The Colleen Moore part of the label looks like a facsimile of her signature.

The dealer's Doll Castle also had a detachable balcony section which was missing from the example pictured in *Dolls' Houses in America*. In our initial correspondence she commented, "This particular piece adds much grace and charm to the structure." Indeed it does. The balcony creates a very realistic resemblance to the real one. Her castle also had one silk-screened window still fastened to the kitchen wall with very small tack nails. The design is similar to the window in the princess' bedroom of the Fairy Castle.

The Doll Castle

Rich Toys

Doll Castle with Eight Rooms

Doll Castle with Five Rooms

Doll Castle with Three Rooms

*"Do you know of a manufactured
version of a famous dollhouse? The only
one we know about is Colleen Moore's
Doll Castle by Rich Toys."*

Dee Snyder, *Nutshell News*, February 1988

Rich Toys

Maurice and Edward Rich were brothers who had a long partnership in various toy and non-toy businesses that primarily involved wood products. They were initially located in Sterling, Illinois in the 1920s. As their business grew, they moved to Morrison, Illinois, and then, in 1935, to Clinton, Iowa, where the Doll Castle was manufactured. By this time their main focus was toy products. They remained in Clinton until 1953, when they moved to Tupelo, Mississippi, where, in 1962, a disastrous flood closed the business. Rich Toys' product line included, besides dollhouses, many styles of horse drawn wagons, forts, trains, garages, barns, etc. One of the most collectible of their wagons is the Borden Milk Wagon.

In a visit to Clinton, Iowa in 1987, I stopped at the library to see if information about Rich Toys might be available. As luck would have it, Denise, the daughter-in-law of Virginia Rich Baker (the daughter of Maurice Rich) was also in the library. I showed her a picture of my Colleen Moore

Doll Castle, and her recollection was that not too many had been made. She had some catalogs but did not remember any reference to it. However, she suggested I call her mother-in-law and gave me her phone number.

I phoned Mrs. Baker and one of her initial comments about the Doll Castle was that "They just didn't sell very well." She felt the traditional Colonial and Tudor style dollhouses were more popular, as were their wagons. Mrs. Baker recalled that the Doll Castle had been available in different sizes, and that all of their dollhouses had to be assembled after purchase. She recollected coming to Chicago to see the real one on display. She gave me the name of her cousin, E. M. Rich, Jr., who lived in a suburb near Chicago. He had been a salesman for Rich Toys and had kept copies of the catalogs.

Upon returning to Chicago, I called Mr. Rich. He was surprised that a Doll Castle still existed but said there were no references to it in any of his catalogs. He thought his Uncle Maurice might have designed it. Mr. Rich had seen the Fairy Castle when it was on display at The Fair and he had met Colleen Moore. He also said that his nieces and nephews were interested in the toys produced by the company.

Rich Toys produced the Doll Castle in three sizes: *height x width x depth*

Eight rooms — 20" x 30" x 19"

Five rooms — 17" x 24" x 23"

Three rooms — 15" x 20-1/2" x 10"

Utilizing the same technique used for producing the company's toy forts, the eight and five-room castles were made with U.S. Gypsum Hardboard and pine pieces. The exterior walls were painted a cream color with grey brick silk-screened details. The roof and the tops of the towers were glossy red, the floor interiors either bright yellow or light green.

The interior walls were left a natural brown except for silk-screened Gothic motifs around the doors and windows. The windows in the bathroom and kitchen were the same size with a silk-screened design similar to the princess' bedroom in the Fairy Castle. The large window in the living room had two black lines from top to bottom spaced to imitate pillars. If you compare the toy version to the real one, it is amazingly representational.

The eight-room Doll Castle also included a courtyard section with two graduated half-moon steps leading from two doorways to a brick walkway. This is shown in the example pictured in Flora Gill Jacobs' book, *Dolls' Houses in America*. In Dee Snyder's article on the Doll Castle in *Nutshell News*, she mentioned a 10" by 8" courtyard.

In spite of the fact that there was limited production of the Doll Castles, and they did not sell well, I have to *believe* that somewhere in a dusty attic there rests a mint-in-box Doll Castle waiting to be rediscovered.

Above: An example of a Rich Fort, which shows the similarity of design and construction to the Doll Castle. A stamped circle on the inside of the fort reads: Clinton, Iowa – Rich Toys – made in U.S.A.

Doll Castle with Eight Rooms

Note: Top floor is missing interior wall at left.

1930s Wyandotte Coupe

A Closer View...

The bathroom window was copied from the original found in the kitchen.

The actual label, still affixed on the Doll Castle with Eight Rooms.
The Colleen Moore part of the label looks like a facsimile of her signature.

Doll Castle with Five Rooms

The five-room version of the Doll Castle (pictures not available) is almost identical to the eight-room castle. The layout of the rooms is three on the first floor and two on the second floor. In the larger castle, there are five rooms on the first floor and three on the second floor. The floors are painted a glossy light green not the bright yellow of the larger castle.

Other differences include a large tower top in the middle of the back of the larger castle, which is not included on the smaller version.

The little towers on the right and left side of the front match each other. On the larger castle this tower is only on the right side. The biggest difference is the balcony. On this version it is neither dimensional nor detachable. The balcony details were silk-screened on the exterior wall.

A picture of the five-room Doll Castle may be found on page 187 of *Toy Buildings 1880-1980* by Patsy Cooper and Dian Zillner, Schiffer Publishing, 2000.

Doll Castle with Three Rooms

The three-room version of the Doll Castle was a surprise. I had always assumed it was made of U.S. Gypsum Hardboard like the larger versions. A recent find by Collectors Sally and Tom McEnteer discovers that it is made of cardboard! They very kindly provided the pictures for this book.

The cardboard Doll Castle is the size shown in The Fair 1935 ad and was sold for $1.00. The McEnteer's example is missing the small towers and a little balcony, which also included a small tower. However, they were delighted to acquire it. Possibly some youthful owner took the towers off so that the Doll Castle looked more like a traditional doll house.

On the front of the cardboard version, there is green shrubbery and glowing green post lights on the courtyard fencing. The interior doorways although Gothic in style do not have the architectural detailing

found in the Gypsum versions, but each room has a large colorful carpet rather than a plain floor.

Across the right side of the cardboard Doll Castle is inscribed "The Official COLLEEN MOORE Doll Castle." Below that in a similar label area as shown on the larger versions are inset the words "A Rich Toy" with line drawings of castle towers on either side.

"King Arthur"
The Castle Cat

Other Toys and Books from The Fair Ad

Colleen Moore's Doll House Cut-Out Book

Colleen Moore's Doll House Storybook

Colleen Moore's Doll House Doll

The Enchanted Castle Book

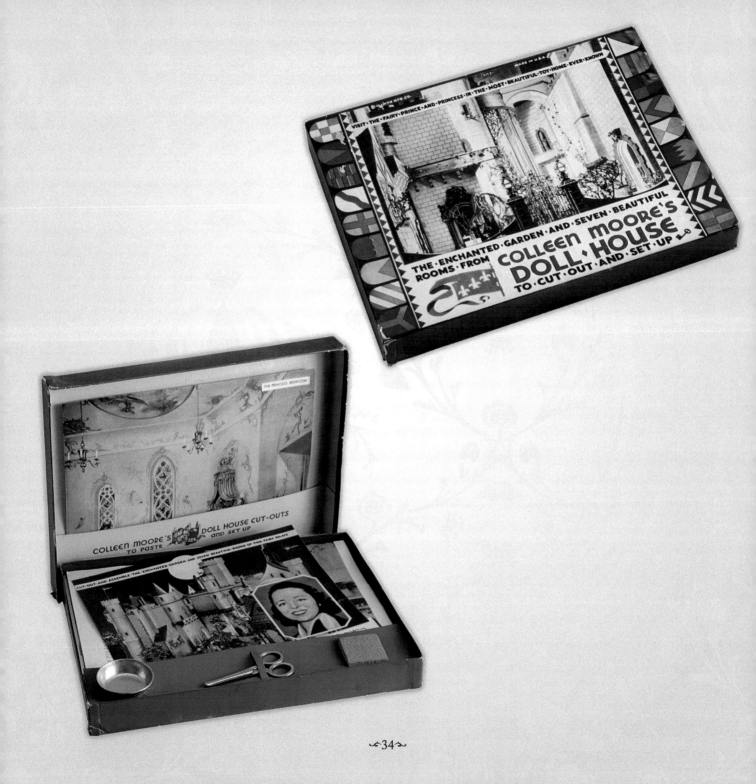

Colleen Moore's Doll House Cut-Out Book

This cut and paste set was made by the Ullman Manufacturing Company of New York and came complete with scissors, sponge and tin dish for water. There are two sheets for each of the seven rooms of the Fairy Castle as well as the Enchanted Garden. One sheet shows the layout and the other gummed sheet has pieces to be cut out, moistened and then put in place on the layout. The individual light cardboard sheets measure 10" by 14" and were for the Kitchen, Dining Hall, Library,

Drawing Room, Princess' Bedroom, Prince's Bedroom, and Chapel.

An additional seven sheets show pictures of the dollhouse with story and text. One shows a picture of Colleen Moore holding this set, and there is a card underneath, in her handwriting, which reads "Wishing you many happy hours of play. Colleen Moore."

On the bottom of the box containing this set is the original price tag of The May Company: $1.00.

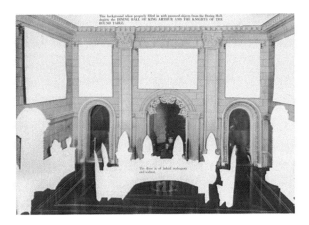

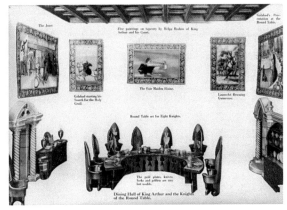

Dining Hall of King Arthur and the Knights of the Round Table

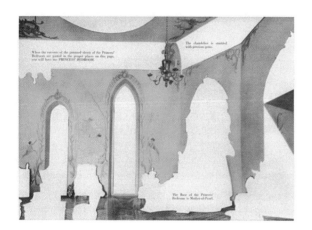 

The Princess' Bedroom

 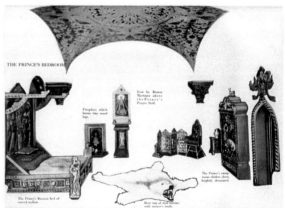

The Prince's Bedroom

Colleen Moore's Doll House Storybook

This booklet was shown in The Fair ad and sold for twenty-five cents. It was published by Garden City Publishing Co., Inc., Garden City, New York, Copyright 1935. Later editions were copyrighted 1935, 1939.

I managed to find one that had been customized for The Fair for Christmas 1935. Miss Moore mentioned in her book *Silent Star* that the Fairy Castle was on display at The Fair for six weeks.

As you look at the pictures of the Fairy Castle rooms in this booklet, compared to more recent photographs, it is obvious that furnishings and accessories were added over the years. Many additional treasures for the Fairy Castle were given to Colleen Moore by family, friends and people she met when she took the castle on tour. Miss Moore, herself, continued to add to its contents.

Colleen Moore's Doll House Doll

The Fair ad shows the Colleen Moore Doll House doll in a cardboard suitcase with two extra dresses and a playsuit. The doll was actually Effanbee's composition Wee Patsy. She wears a round tin pin, red background and a yellow heart, on which is inscribed "Colleen Moore Fairy Princess an Eff-an-Bee Doll." Without the pin, she is just a mere Wee Patsy. The doll is 5-1/2" tall and too large for most dollhouses, particularly the Rich Toy Doll Castle.

The Fairy Princess also came in a small box measuring 3" by 6" by 1-1/2." The colorful graphics mimic a castle, and the box is marked Fairy Princess Doll in bold letters and has the heart-shaped trademark with the words "An Eff-an-Bee Durable Doll." The window above the castle door on the box is perforated so when the doll was in the box it opened to show her face. On the back of the box is "The Story of Fairy Princess – The Colleen Moore Doll House Doll."

My Fairy Princess is dressed in white net, trimmed with pink silk ribbon over pink organdy with attached lace trimmed panties. She proudly wears her Fairy Princess pin. This is the same outfit illustrated on the inside lid of the cardboard suitcase which contained the Fairy Princess as illustrated in The Fair ad. The lid also shows The Story of Fairy Princess.

The brand-name Effanbee is actually an acronym for the Fleischaker & Baum doll company which was founded in New York City around 1910. One of their most successful line of dolls was the "Patsy" in the late 1920s and 1930s. The Wee Patsy was the smallest member.

The back of the Fairy Princess doll box, enlarged so that you can read the Story of Fairy Princess. Box shown actual size.

The text on the box reads:

The Story of
FAIRY PRINCESS
THE COLLEEN MOORE
DOLL HOUSE DOLL

Colleen Moore, the famous moving picture actress, has been very fond of dolls all her life. She has just built the most wonderful doll house you ever saw. It is truly a fairy castle, with its lovely golden walls and its exquisite doll furniture.

And Colleen Moore wanted a wonderful doll to live in such a wonderful doll house. So she naturally choose an EFFanBEE doll. We made Fairy Princess, the Colleen Moore Doll House Doll, especially for her. She was so delighted with it, so entranced with the lovely features and the charming dress of Fairy Princess, that she immediately chose it as the Official Doll for her doll house.

Now you, too, can enjoy playing with this Fairy Princess Doll. Just think of the fun you can have! She is an EFFanBEE Durable Doll, which means that you can play with her and sew for her, ever so many pretty frocks.

The Enchanted Castle Book

Colleen Moore wrote this storybook about two little girls who find a fairy ring in the grass and soon are only four inches tall and transported to a storybook land. The book was published by Garden City Publishing Company in 1935 and was part of the promotion as shown in The Fair ad.

The book was illustrated by Marie A. Lawson. Many of the illustrations echo the rooms of the Fairy Castle, although in the book they are inhabited by fairytale characters like Cinderella, Captain Kidd, Peter Pan and Little Bo Peep, to name a few. There is also a prince who has been turned into a big cuddly bear. Mr. Rudytoot, the King's Bugler, is the little girls' guide through this kingdom.

In the June 1987 issue of *Collectors Miniature Exchange*, for which I wrote an article about the Rich Toy Doll Castle, fellow collector Betty Schult shared a letter she had received from Colleen Moore with regard to this storybook.

Miss Moore wrote that "The idea for the story was an old one with me. As a child, I used to dream of being made tiny, just as in the book, and having a trip to a fairy castle. When I was eight, I used to gather the children in the neighborhood around me and tell them this story. I suppose this is really the background of the building of my Fairy Castle."

Miss Moore also mentioned that the two little girls in the book, Bebe and Jean, to whom the book is dedicated, were second cousins and that her mother wrote all the jingles.

At the end of the storybook, each of the little girls was given a golden heart on which is engraved…

"Always believe in fairies."

Related Items

Tootsietoy Doll House Furnishings

Colleen Moore's 3D Dimension Magic Theatre

Durable Toy and Novelty Corporation
Colleen Moore's Enchanted Castle in Six Reels

Tootsietoy Doll House Furnishings

One of the most whimsical brand names in the history of toys is Tootsietoy, made by the Dowst Manufacturing Company of Chicago. The company's early success with a miniature metal iron laundry premium and metal Cracker Jack toys led to their die-cast product line in the 1920s. Small cars, trucks, boats, planes and trains were available for little boys; doll house furniture and cardboard doll houses were a delight for little girls. Many of these products came in colorful boxes which have become almost as collectible as the contents.

The Tootsietoy box pictured with the castle in the background, was undoubtedly used during the Colleen Moore toy promotion. Scale-wise, 1/2 inch, it was the most colorful and appropriate furniture available for the size of the rooms in the Rich Toy Doll Castle.

The first Tootsietoy doll furnishings were made in the 1920s and sold in small boxed sets. In 1930, Dowst introduced a new line which was more colorful and more evocative of the real furniture of the era. There were overstuffed sofas and chairs, Hoosier cabinets and Kelvinator refrigerators, enclosed bathtubs, patterned and flocked tin bedspreads and chaise lounges in the bedrooms.

1920s Bedroom Set

More significantly, the drawers now opened as did the cabinet doors; even the oven opened. A magnificent grand piano was added to the line and it too opened to show the gold string interior. Surprisingly, neither the 1920s nor 1930s line of Tootsietoy furniture included a nursery set.

The sets also came in a colorful box marked "New Tootsietoy Furniture." On the cover were fairies and children with the new pieces of furniture. Many of these sets later came with small metal accessories. The bedroom and living room each had six items. The kitchen and dining room each had ten items. Some of the dining room items were a coffee pot, goblet, covered pedestal dish, pitcher, cups and saucers, candy dishes and candelabra.

During the 1930s, Dowst also marketed the 1920 line under the brand name "Daisy." One of the Daisy boxes also has a castle in the background. The raised Tootsietoy logo on the furnishings was covered over and the sets sold for less than the usual $1.00.

To furnish the Doll Castle, I primarily used Tootsietoy's 1930 product line. The bedroom set was now available in three versions: basic, boudoir (with the addition of a chaise lounge and vanity dresser) and guest room. Bedspreads were removable and came in patterned or flocked tin.

Another addition to the new product line was a music room, which featured the grand piano and cabinet radio.

From the 1920s, I used Tootsietoy's stately "gold" living room set to furnish the side parlor as shown below.

"Small cars, trucks, boats, planes and trains were available for little boys; doll house furniture and cardboard doll houses were a delight for little girls."

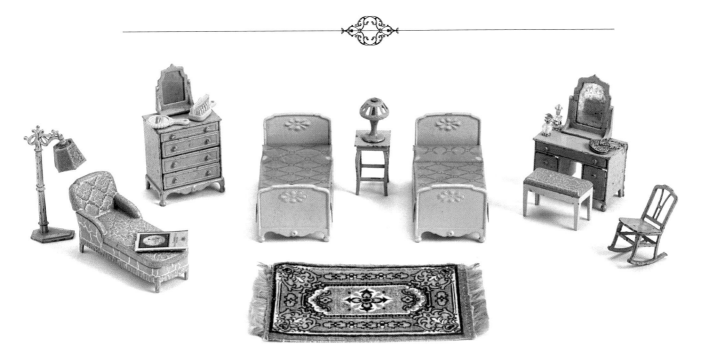

Colleen Moore's 3D Magic Theatre

A film strip of the Fairy Castle, as it was furnished in 1935, came with a cardboard box viewer; you ran the film strip through the box, looking through the eye holes to see each room. A booklet came with the box that described each of the nineteen scenes. It also came in a small cube-shaped box called the Monocular Viewer.

It seems apropos that a film strip starring Colleen Moore's Doll House in a Magic Theatre would be produced as another merchandising tie-in.

Views of the World
Diamond D Studios

Bedford Bldg. Chicago
U.S. Pat. No. 2071120
Copyright 1936

Measures 5-3/4" wide,
3-3/8" height, 1-1/2" deep

Durable Toy and Novelty Corporation

200 Fifth Avenue, New York, Room 104

Set No. 90 features six reels of Colleen Moore's Enchanted Castle

• How to Make the Enchanted Castle, 2 reels

• How to Make the Rooms of the Enchanted Castle, 2 reels

• Bobby and Jeanne's visit to the Enchanted Castle, 2 reels

Viewing these reels requires an Uncle Sam's Movie projector, which I have never found. The reel strips look like colorful cartoons, and on each reel box is noted "Animated Film."

Instructions on the box describe how to make your own drawings and cutouts with the projector and tracer. It appears that you ran the reel through the lighted projector which would enlarge the image on a table. The movie projector also had a Durotone Talkie System.

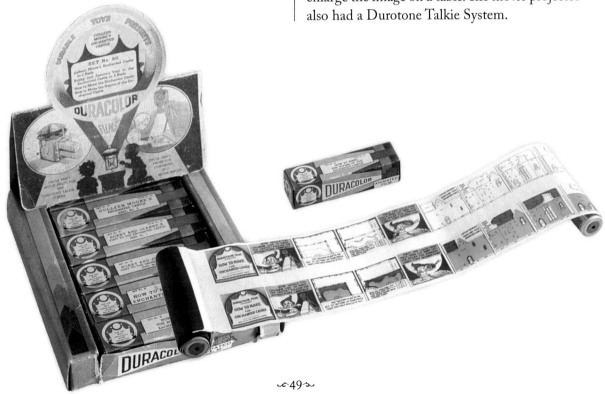

Making the
Doll Castle a Home

Doll Castle Dolls

Castle Carpets

Accessories

Doll Castle Dolls

Since Rich Toys called their version of the Fairy Castle the Doll Castle, I thought it only fitting that many small-size dolls should grace the premises.

Scale-wise, the 3" to 3-1/2" all-bisque, wire-jointed dolls, made in Germany in the 1920s, with their molded Dutch-bob flapper hairdos and hand-painted faces were most appropriate. "Germany" is incised on the backs of the larger dolls and on the arms of the smaller dolls.

Over the years, I have been able to collect more than twenty of these dolls, including a 3-3/4" maid who resides in the dining room preparing punch and sandwiches for an afternoon doll party.

All but one of these dolls are dressed in their original outfits. Felt, gauzy and small patterned fabrics were used in fashioning their clothes; many still wear their felt cloche hats. Beads were used for buttons, rayon ribbon for bows, and a few have tiny metal belt buckles. They all wear the popular Mary Jane style low-heeled one strap shoes.

There are some exceptions: one doll has a molded cloche, another a molded non-flapper hairdo with a molded bow, and several have a widow's peak in the hairdo. The maid's cap is molded into the hairdo.

The Dutch-bob hairstyle was made very popular by Colleen Moore in the 1923 film *Flaming Youth*.

Castle Carpets

During the many years I was collecting dollhouses, I always felt that the more accessories you added, such as pictures, dishes, food, rugs, etc., along with small-size dolls, the more charming and interesting the dollhouse became.

The easiest items to find for the Doll Castle were the miniature Oriental rugs which had been given as a premium with the purchase of cigarettes in the early 20th century. I used them throughout the Doll Castle, even in the bathroom. The rugs measure 2-1/4" by 3-1/2" or 3" by 4." The small rugs were printed on fabric with a velour finish with matching silky fringe.

Many of the smaller rugs are stamped on the back:

The Original Rug

Luxury Cigarettes

Factory No. 7 3rd

Dist. of N.Y.

Patent License No. 1045372

Accessories

What makes a doll house so fascinating is all the tiny accessories that make it look like a real home. Since Tootsietoy furnishings are half-inch in scale, it was a challenge to find vintage or appropriate contemporary miniatures reminiscent of the 1930s.

As we tour the rooms of the Doll Castle, some noteworthy items can be seen. In the Hoosier cabinet in the kitchen are four miniature cans of Heinz products: Cooked Macaroni, Oven Baked Beans, Tomato Juice, and Home Style Soup. These little cans came from a charm bracelet fastened to a card marked "Atlantic City – 1940." Most likely it was a promotional giveaway. Other advertising charms are a can of Pet Milk, also in the kitchen, and a can of Dutch Cleanser in the bathroom. There is also a vintage copper toaster in the kitchen; the sides open down to show red toasting coils!

The dining room contains two other vintage copper miniatures: a coffee urn and a handled tray. There is also a pair of brass candlestick holders.

On the library tables in the living room are a collection of miniature Roseville Pottery vases decorated with flower designs from the 1930s and '40s. A portrait of Colleen Moore in a blue dress hangs on the back wall. This painting originally hung in her Bel Air Mansion in California and a small version is in the Fairy Castle. On the piano are miniature copies of sheet music from two Colleen Moore films: *Sally* and *Smiling Irish Eyes*.

A catalog provided 1930 reproduction vintage posters mostly from the Chicago area in just the right size to adorn the walls of the Doll Castle. Two from the "1933 Century of Progress" held in Chicago are hanging in the parlor. An opera poster of *Madame Butterfly* hangs in the green bedroom.

Over the years I have collected Colleen Moore memorabilia including many movie studio photos. Small framed copies of these photos may be found in some of the rooms. I also made miniature copies of her two books: *Silent Star* and *The Enchanted Castle*. Adding these accessories to the rooms was a way to truly make this Colleen Moore's Doll Castle.

Accessories shown to scale.

Contemporary miniature Roseville Pottery
by Jeanetta Kendall.

EL RANCHITO

Ph. (805) 434-1424
Route 2, Box 207-A
Templeton, Calif. 93465

August 11, 1986

Ms. Carol Stevenson
416 North Humphrey
Oak Park, Illinois 60302

Dear Ms. Stevenson:

Your letter was most interesting and it
is always a great pleasure to hear from
another miniature collector because we
each know the joy our hobby has given
to us.

I am sorry I cannot write my name
smaller, but I have a very serious eye
problem and it is difficult to see.

Good luck with your autographs. I had
great fun collecting mine.

Sincerely,

Colleen Moore

Colleen Moore Maginot

CMM/bl

Another interesting facet of the Colleen Moore Fairy Castle is an autograph book containing signatures of many famous people of the 20th Century: six presidents, Eleanor Roosevelt, Frank Lloyd Wright, Queen Elizabeth, Henry Ford, Picasso, Albert Einstein, and Toscanini, to name a few. Her 1971 book *Colleen Moore's Doll House* has a delightful chapter devoted to the stories behind collecting these autographs.

Shortly after I acquired the toy version, I was pondering how to contact Colleen Moore when I found a letter from her in the booklet for the National Association of Miniature Enthusiasts National House Party being held in Chicago in August 1986. The letter gave Miss Moore's home address.

I wrote to her and told her about my treasure and explained how I would appreciate her autograph for my Doll Castle. I enclosed a miniature autograph book. Shortly thereafter, the small book came back not only autographed but with the very gracious note shown above.

Bibliography

Ackerman, Evelyn. *Dolls in Miniature.*
Gold Horse Publishing, a Division of Theriault's, 1991.

Ferguson, Candee. "Colleen Moore Doll Castle reigns at toy museum."
Antique Trader's Collector Magazine and Price Guide. December 2001, 11-16.

Jacobs, Flora Gill. *Dolls' Houses in America.* New York: Charles Scribner's Sons, 1974, 80-81.

Moore, Colleen. *Silent Star.* New York: Doubleday & Company, 1968.

Moore, Colleen. *Colleen Moore's Doll House.* New York: Doubleday & Company, 1971.

Moyer, Patsy. "A Castle for a Fairy Princess." *Patsy and Friends Newsletter.* December 1988, 12-15.

Neff, Terry Ann R., *Within the Fairy Castle.* Boston: Little, Brown and Company, 1997.

Snyder, Dee. "Colleen Moore's Doll Castle by Rich Toys." *Nutshell News,* February 1988, 36-37.

Snyder, Dee. "Cigarette Premium Rugs." *Nutshell News,* June 1987, 32-33.

Stevenson, Carol. "A Wish Come True." *Collectors Miniature Exchange,* June 1987.

Zillner, Dian. *American Dollhouses and Furnishings from the 20th Century.*
Atglen, PA: Schiffer Publishing, 1985.

Zillner, Dian. *Dollhouse And Furniture Advertising. 1880s-1980s,*
Atglen, PA: Schiffer Publishing, 2004.

Photo Credits

Movie studio photos of Colleen Moore, pages 4 and 52, from the author's collection.

Photos of the three-room Colleen Moore Doll Castle, pages 30 and 31,
photographed by Tom McEnteer.

About the Author

Carol Stevenson, a native Chicagoan, started collecting dollhouses and toys in the 1970s. At that time, she also became a member of the Wee "c" Miniature Club in the Chicago area, as well as a member of the National Association of Miniature Enthusiasts.

Two of her favorite creations are a Turn-of-the-Century Marshall Field's Department Store and the Rose and Crown Inn, located in England, which is a part of her family history. A mug rack in the pub area of the inn serves as a family tree. On each mug is inscribed the first name of an ancestor. During 1974, Carol also made doll house accessories for Marshall Field's Toy Department.

Her childhood dollhouse from the 1940s was a Colonial Mansion by Rich Toys. It came filled with wooden Strombecker furnishings and handmade curtains and bedspreads from her mother. The wood furnishings were replaced with plastic Renwal when they became available at the local Woolworth's after World War II.

Carol divides her time between Chicago and Mineral Point, Wisconsin. In 1997, she opened the Mineral Point Toy Museum to display and share her collection. The museum was closed in 2007, but many photographs of the toys from the collection are shown in the book *Toy Buildings 1880-1980* by Patty Cooper and Dian Zillner.

*The princess' bedroom in the Fairy Castle
contains a window similar to the only remaining
window in the kitchen of the Doll Castle.*

The End